701 Things That P*ss Me Off About Work

701 Things That P*ss Me Off About Work

I. M. Peeved with Ed Strnad

❖ ❖ ❖ ❖ ❖

Developed by The Philip Lief Group, Inc.

A Perigee Book

A Perigee Book
Published by The Berkley Publishing Group
200 Madison Avenue
New York, NY 10016

Published by arrangement with The Philip Lief Group, Inc.,
6 West 20th Street, New York, NY 10011.

Copyright © 1996 by The Philip Lief Group, Inc.
Book design by Maureen Troy
Cover design by Joe Lanni

First edition: September 1996

Published simultaneously in Canada.

The Putnam Berkley World Wide Web site address is
http://www.berkley.com

Library of Congress Cataloging-in-Publication Data
Peeved, I. M.
     701 things that p*ss me off about work / I. M. Peeved
with Ed Strnad ; developed by the Philip Lief Group, Inc.
        p.   cm.
     ISBN 0-399-52231-x
     I. Strnad, Ed.   II. Philip Lief Group.   III. Title.
PN6162.P353   1996
818'.5402—dc20
                                                        96-5344
                                                           CIP

Printed in the United States of America

10 9 8 7 6 5 4 3 2 1

$\mathcal{A}$cknowledgments

No one—the author did the work all by himself. Well, maybe his editor, Kelli Daley, helped a little. Okay, and Gary M. Krebs, too, but that's it. Oh, yeah—JoAnn Strnad, also. True, George Zarr's work was laughable. And Grandma's work—though the author didn't appreciate it earlier—is now remembered with fondness & gratitude.

—E.S.   *KGNJ65A@prodigy.com*

Introduction

Monday morning, back to work . . . these are the most dreaded words in English. Why does work tick off so many people? I'm glad you asked. This book lists 701 reasons that will answer many of your vexing questions, like why you hit the "snooze" button eighteen times every weekday morning.

How do you know if work jostles your giblets? Take this simple quiz to find out.

Which annoys you more?
- (a) That today you need a four-year degree just to flip burgers
- (b) That Andy Rooney gets paid for what he does
- (c) That the dork at the next desk *loves* to pop bubble-wrap, or
- (d) All of the above, damn it . . . *I need a vacation!*

If you answered a, b, c, or d, you need this book *desperately.*

But why do millions hate work? There are four main reasons:

1. Work is disappointing. When you were a child, what did you want to be when you grew up? Don't tell me you always dreamed of becoming "the Western Regional Manager for Amalgamated Weed Whacker," or fantasized about being a certified public accountant. Admit it: you've had to lower your expectations by a few zillion miles.

2. Work is thankless. Like the old song asked, "Sixteen tons, and what do you get?" (Answer: a hernia.) You followed all the rules, played the game, and sold your soul only to be reorganized, downsized, burnt out, put out to pasture, laid off, riffed, and summarily dismissed. And that was just your summer job!

3. Work is fickle. George Bush lost his job; Saddam Hussein still has his. Go figure.

4. Work sucks. It just *does.* Big time. It drains the life force clean out of you. Take my word for it.

Then why do people work? Easy: paychecks are *addictive.* Nicotine's got nothing on them. After a few deposits in your bank account, you'll do *anything* for one. I wrote this book for a paycheck—*if possible, don't let it happen to you!*

701 Things That P*ss Me Off About Work is the definitive collection of work-related injuries and insults to your psyche. (However, do *not* apply for Worker's Compensation on the basis of anything in this book; I doubt insulted psyches are covered.) It will guide you safely through today's treacherous Not-So-Brave New World of Work; it will give you something to read during boring meetings; it will pay my rent. Now, get back to work. And don't pop that bubble-wrap.

—I. M. Peeved

Monday mornings

❖

Having to "look busy"

❖

When the high point of
your day is lunch

Alarm clocks with
no snooze button

❖

Cubicles

❖

Crotchety old-timers
who carp that you make more
than they do

Obnoxious young morons
who make more money
than you do

❖

Being watched by
a security camera
while you work

Chucking the nine-to-five
to start your own business and
working eight-to-eight

❖

Leaving for work when it's
still dark outside

Fighting the morning traffic jam

❖

Fighting the evening traffic jam

❖

Offices with piped-in Muzak

*G*oing to work with too
little sleep and dragging yourself
through the day

❖

*H*olidays in the middle
of the week

When your printer's last
cartridge runs dry in the
middle of a rush job

❖

"Please hold"

Staples that break apart as you are
putting them in the stapler

❖

Administrative assistants who take
offense at being called "secretaries"
but who nonetheless expect
to be taken to lunch for
Professional Secretaries Day

Discovering it's lonely at the top—but even lonelier at the middle

❖

Bosses who quip, "Are you working hard, or hardly working?"

$\mathcal{B}$eing unable to find the on-ramp
to the fast track

❖

$\mathcal{F}$alling off the fast track

❖

$\mathcal{H}$itting the "glass ceiling"

Typists with
Dracula-length fingernails

❖

Small pay raises that just nudge you
into a higher tax bracket

$\mathcal{N}$ever reaching a live human being
when you call another business

❖

$\mathcal{W}$hen your going-away party is
held at a Jack in the Box

When the boss catches you doing
the daily crossword puzzle

❖

Employees who say, "I don't know,
I only work here"

Coworkers who insist,
"I'm just doing this until I can sell
my screenplay/script/musical"

❖

When people advise you,
"Don't quit your day job"

$\mathcal{N}$ot doing what you love

❖

$\mathcal{W}$hen doing what you love
doesn't pay the bills

❖

$\mathcal{N}$eeding two incomes to pay
your mortgage

$\mathcal{G}$uilt over putting your
kids in day care

❖

$\mathcal{T}$he Peter Principle:
that people are promoted past
their level of competence

*P*arkinson's Law:
how work always expands/contracts
to fill the time available

❖

*B*eing the teeny little box
at the bottom of the
"org chart"

$\mathcal{W}$aiting years for the person
above you to quit, get fired,
be promoted, or die

❖

$\mathcal{W}$hen the receptionist announces
that you have a personal call
over the intercom

When someone makes
hand shadows with the
overhead projector during
your presentation

❖

Having to declare
your tips to the I.R.S.

Relentlessly upbeat company
newsletters that tow the
management line

❖

Being occupationally typecast;
e.g., "The Computer Guy,"
"The Shipping Person,"
"Our Accounts Receivable
People," etc.

$\mathcal{N}$ot recalling ever wanting to be a "Supervisor of Quality Assurance" when you were a kid

❖

$\mathcal{W}$orking as a temp

$\mathcal{W}$orking in the
Complaint Department

❖

$\mathcal{W}$hen you're a "day person"
on the night shift

❖

$\mathcal{F}$reezes on wages and salaries

$\mathcal{P}$erpetually grinning salespeople

❖

$\mathcal{W}$hen the management plays
quick-paced music in an attempt
to make you work faster

People who ask
"What do you do?"
the moment you meet

❖

Holding any job that
involves phlegm or sputum

Sweatshops

❖

Piecework

❖

Workaholics

Mugs and T-shirts imprinted with
motivational slogans; e.g.,
"Zero Defects!" . . .
"We Care!" . . .
"Get Back to Work!"

❖

"Team (company name)"
(e.g., Team Xerox)

Bottom-line mentalities

❖

When coworkers advise you to slow down because you're making them look bad

Workers afraid of rocking the boat
and making waves

❖

The illusion of job security

❖

Overflowing "In" boxes

$\mathcal{W}$hen it's a dirty job,
and you're the one who has to do it

❖

$\mathcal{R}$eally dirty jobs,
like cesspool cleaner,
road-kill remover, etc.

❖

$\mathcal{T}$oo-short maternity leaves

$\mathcal{W}$orking harder and harder
just to stay where you are

❖

$\mathcal{W}$hen word of your
imminent layoff comes through
the grapevine

$\mathcal{I}$nvesting work and money in an enterprise that goes belly-up

❖

$\mathcal{W}$earing a pager that keeps you at everyone's beck and call

Employees who think that just showing up for work entitles them to frequent pay increases and rapid promotions

❖

When your manager considers you a "subordinate"

Staff meetings

❖

Assembly lines

❖

Never getting to touch
the finished product

Companies that keep tabs on
what you do outside of work

❖

When you have the
Seven Work Habits of
Highly Ineffective People

Business ethics and
other oxymorons

❖

Paycuts

❖

Papercuts

Pink slips

❖

Demotions

❖

Retirees at a loss for
something useful to do

When your department is
cut in half but has to do the
same amount of work

❖

When the fruits of your
labor taste sour

Having to jump through hoops
to please your boss

❖

Employees who are chronically
four or five minutes late

When the new job requires you
to be able to walk on water,
leap tall buildings in a single bound,
be all things to all people, etc.

❖

Constantly fearing that someone
will discover you're just a big kid
dressed in grown-up work clothes

Skipping lunch

❖

No time for daydreaming

❖

Taking work home with you

$\mathcal{A}$lways feeling like Sisyphus,
pushing that rock up the hill

❖

$\mathcal{W}$hen someone dies on the job
in a bizarre manner,
like drowning in a vat of molasses

Having to explain employment
gaps on your resume to a
potential employer

❖

That teachers only have to work
nine months a year

That Santa Claus only has to
work one night a year

❖

Twelve-hour shifts

❖

Unpaid overtime

Not being able to tell off-color jokes
in the office anymore

❖

People who don't consider
homemaking and child raising
real work

$\mathcal{W}$hen coworkers manipulate
the data to get the results they want

❖

$\mathcal{W}$orking all day, then coming
home and "working" on
your relationship with your
S.O., kids, etc.

Efficiency experts who
time how long you take on
a bathroom break

❖

Being afraid to follow
your talent to the strange places
it will lead you

The niggling feeling that you should be doing something else with your life

❖

Making a midlife career change

People whose jobs entail
designing more efficient ways
to blow people up

❖

When too many people in your
department take vacation
simultaneously

Airless offices

❖

Tuneless whistling
from the next cubicle

Coming home after your kids
have gone to sleep

❖

Knowing that Social Security
will not be around by
the time you retire

Running out of energy every day
around 2:00 P.M.

❖

When inferior products are
shipped in order to meet a deadline

$\mathcal{W}$hen office-supply stores
charge businesses much more than
they charge ordinary consumers

❖

$\mathcal{B}$elieving that you are
what you do for a living

"Stress" interviews

❖

Being replaced by a machine

❖

Being replaced by a younger person

$\mathcal{W}$orking for a jerk

❖

$\mathcal{W}$orking for a jerk when
you're self-employed

Trying to get to work in
two feet of snow

❖

Finding the office is closed on
account of weather after you arrive

$\mathcal{N}$ever having a "snow day" in L.A.

❖

$\mathcal{W}$hen your hobby becomes your job and ceases to be fun anymore

Having to make inane conversation
with the guy whose desk is next
to the copy machine

❖

Becoming programmed by your
alarm clock so that you wake up
the same time each morning,
even on weekends and vacations

Having to drive more than thirty
minutes to get to your job

❖

When your boss won't help you
get out of jury duty

$\mathcal{W}$hen your expense account
gets cut

❖

$\mathcal{R}$ules against horseplay

$\mathcal{B}$eing suspended without pay

❖

$\mathcal{W}$hen your work doesn't
make a difference

Rules against decorating
your cubicle

❖

Union rules that prohibit you from
cleaning your own desk

When your personality
clashes with the boss's

❖

People who play pranks
with the P.A. system

When companies bemoan the lack of employee loyalty, but lay off people at the drop of a hat

❖

Business leaders fixated on short-term results

"The customer is always right"

❖

Gender-free job titles;
e.g., fisherperson, server,
mail carrier, etc.

Being kept on hold for eons
when you're calling from
your cellular phone

❖

Employees who have to be
retrained every Monday

Getting shunted onto
the "mommy track"

❖

When you get docked pay for
staying home with your sick child

Not earning enough to be able to afford a house like your parents'

❖

Not being able to stay at home to see your kids grow up like your mom did

"Empowerment" and other
trendy, empty buzzwords

❖

Being a fifty-year-old bellboy

When your mate works nights and you work days, and you pass each other like ships in the night

❖

Being overqualified for your job

The job requirement that says
traffic-light timers must possess
a sadistic sense of humor

❖

When your blood pressure
is the only thing that gets
a raise at your job

*N*ot knowing the difference between
a vocation and an avocation

❖

*P*eople who get ahead without
paying their dues

When you say something
in a meeting, it's ignored, then
someone else says the same thing
and everyone thinks it's
a brilliant idea

❖

Reaching a dead end
on your career path

$\mathcal{W}$hen a *60 Minutes* news crew is
waiting in your office for you

❖

$\mathcal{B}$eing "working class" in a
supposedly class-free society

❖

$\mathcal{F}$orgetting your I.D. badge

Having to break in a new boss

❖

When the new boss is the
same as the old boss

❖

When your boss quotes Machiavelli

$\mathcal{E}$mployees who wear ties to
the company picnic

❖

$\mathcal{T}$he first day back to work
after your vacation

❖

$\mathcal{G}$oing through your voice-mail
messages after a two-week vacation

When things mysteriously
disappear from your desk,
then mysteriously reappear

❖

When everyone takes credit for a
successful project

When the guilty parties
distance themselves from
their failed project

❖

Whistle-blowers

When a woman is told she
thinks like a man

❖

Having to network with
people you detest

The old-boy network

❖

When the last shift doesn't
tell the new shift what they
need to know

❖

People who step all over
you to get ahead

Being unkind to people on your way up, then meeting them again on your way down

❖

Getting a reputation as a
"company man"

$\mathcal{B}$eing given a cheap plastic award
for an idea that saved the
company millions

❖

$\mathcal{W}$hen awards are given for
expected behavior; e.g.,
attendance, punctuality,
courtesy, etc.

When your secretary tells people
the real reason you're unavailable
(late, out sick, in restroom, etc.)

❖

Trying to devise fool-proof
work procedures when fools
are so ingenious

$\mathcal{G}$etting passed over for a promotion

❖

$\mathcal{H}$aving to put out fires daily when
you aren't a firefighter

❖

$\mathcal{W}$ishing you could eschew
the dog-eat-dog corporate world

Hole punchers that
make misaligned holes

❖

Burning out

❖

Career crashes

Having to ask "How high?" when
the boss says "Jump"

❖

Waiting for the ax to fall

❖

Being the low man (or woman)
on the totem pole

The seniority system

❖

Extended out-of-town business trips

❖

Feeling like the illiterate foreigner
you are on a trip to another country

When "motivationally challenged"
is used to describe someone
who's lazy

❖

Jobs where you have to
deal with the public

❖

That you can't slam cellular phones

$\mathcal{E}$xecutives who drive
ostentatious cars to work

❖

$\mathcal{T}$he fact that women make only
seventy-one cents for every dollar
a man in a comparable job earns

$\mathcal{P}$eople habitually late
for the car pool

❖

$\mathcal{O}$n-the-job training for doctors

❖

$\mathcal{W}$orking with smart-alecky
"rocket scientists"

Never having a mentor

❖

When the office practical joker
covers the toilet bowls
with Saran Wrap

❖

When at first you don't
succeed . . . giving up

𝒫eople who don't consider
jobs in the arts (musician, etc.)
real jobs

❖

𝒫eople who think that
humor writers rake in the big bucks

The inverse relationship between
money and a job's "fun factor":
i.e., the more fun a job is,
the less it pays, and vice versa

❖

When you come in late,
wearing a suit, and everyone
assumes you had an interview
for a new job

Company policies that dictate
women can't wear pants

❖

Fellow employees who partied
while you were going to
school at night and then resent
your promotion

$\mathcal{D}$ry cleaners, banks, and other
businesses that are open only when
working people can't get to them

❖

$\mathcal{W}$hen the anniversary of
your hiring is not celebrated
or even acknowledged

When lavish going-away parties
are thrown for people who are
quitting their jobs

❖

Having to pass people golfing
on your drive to work

Arriving late on a rainy day
and having to park at the far end
of the parking lot

❖

Those bumper stickers
with the too-clever
occupational/sexual suggestions;
e.g., "Electricians do it without
shorts," "Photographers do it
in the dark," etc.

No Thanksgiving turkeys given
away free at work anymore

❖

No Christmas bonuses anymore

When the media name your
place of employment one of
"The Fifty Worst Places to
Work in America"

❖

Having to take a pre-employment
psychological test

That you can flunk a drug test
from eating a poppy-seed bagel

❖

Businesses that try to be the
first name in the phone book; e.g.,
"AAA Aardvark X-ray Supplies"

Becoming a boss and having to buy aspirin and antacid in bulk

❖

That one "Ah, shoot" cancels out one hundred "Atta-boys"

Antisocial people who always
eat lunch at their desks

❖

Discovering an embarrassing
mistake in your memo after you've
mailed out one hundred copies

Having to spend a bright
spring day cooped up
in a stuffy office

❖

Trying to strike a balance
between work and home life

$\mathcal{T}$rying to find the
fastest route home

❖

$\mathcal{W}$hen you could shoot a cannon
through the office at 5:01

$\mathcal{P}$eople who say they're "between jobs" instead of "unemployed"

❖

$\mathcal{E}$mployees who reinvent the wheel every day

When you stop killing time and
time starts killing *you*

❖

Fearing that you'll be
found slumped over your
imitation-wood desk someday

Deadlines

❖

Waiting for
"the eagle to fly" on Friday

Getting one less
paycheck in February

❖

People with bogus job titles,
like "Creative Consultant"

$\mathcal{P}$eers and employees who'd
like nothing better than to
see you screw up

❖

$\mathcal{W}$hen someone links all your
paper clips into a long chain

❖

$\mathcal{W}$ork involving lard

Working for Ross Perot

❖

Getting yelled at the moment
you walk into work

❖

People who start to unwind about
two hours before quitting time

Business books with
"Excellence" in the title

❖

Discovering that achieving
your dreams involves some work

❖

The low-lifes inhabiting
middle management

That the view never changes if
you're not the "lead dog"

❖

Working like a dog,
when dogs actually have
it pretty easy

❖

Coworkers who tattle
on you to the boss

Being driven by work instead
of being driven to work

❖

Discovering the ugly side of a
glitzy profession after you struggle
for years to break into it

The punchline:
"What, and quit my job in
show business?!?"

❖

People who win the rat race
by becoming one

❖

Work-induced nervous breakdowns

$\mathcal{P}$eople who want to "have it all"

❖

$\mathcal{C}$utthroat jobs where a "friend"
is someone who stabs
you in the face

Monetary definitions of success

❖

That there are many people
waiting tables who would have been
excellent ballet dancers

When competition brings out
the best in products and
the worst in people

❖

Worker-motivation posters

$\mathcal{P}$ainfully true office humor
("The beatings will continue until
morale improves")

❖

$\mathcal{W}$hen the computers go
down and you have to use
your brain all day

That sperm donors get paid
for what they do

❖

That Andy Rooney gets paid
for what he does

Business books written by
ivory-tower academics

❖

Consultants who run their own
businesses into the ground,
then charge you big bucks to
show you how to do it

Having to look for a new job
after the office Christmas party

❖

Working in a sausage factory,
knowing what goes into them

Realizing that a baker gets tired of
eating doughnuts eventually

❖

When there's white-out on
your computer screen

$\mathcal{T}$hat the interview for the job
of parenting is too damn easy

❖

$\mathcal{W}$hen you're assigned a secretary
of the same gender

❖

$\mathcal{B}$eing told to clean out your desk

$\mathcal{E}$xit interviews

❖

$\mathcal{W}$hen your most frequently used
computer language is "#!%@&*!!"

❖

$\mathcal{W}$hen the dead come back
to life at five o'clock

Going broke buying
get-rich-quick schemes

❖

"Flavor of the month"
management techniques

❖

People who dress for success

People who undress for success

❖

Having to work two jobs
to make ends meet

❖

People who carry nothing but
their lunch in their briefcases

Having your paycheck garnished

❖

Company policies that mandate that
everyone be on a first-name basis

❖

Illegible notes on your
desk marked "Urgent"

$\mathcal{A}$ memo from the big boss
marked "SEE ME ASAP"

❖

$\mathcal{W}$hen no one meets you at the
airport gate after a trip

❖

$\mathcal{B}$usinesses that allow employees
to come to work in costume
on Halloween

Getting a bank loan from someone
dressed like a clown

❖

Getting shot down on
your rise to the top

❖

When your company gives everyone
a power failure–proof clock radio

$\mathcal{D}$reams about stuff
that happened at work

❖

$\mathcal{L}$osing everything you just
typed on the computer

❖

$\mathcal{A}$lways being the first one in and
having to brew the coffee

Hearing someone typing on a PC
before you get to work

❖

Gussied-up job titles;
e.g., "Sanitation Engineer"
(garbage collector),
and "Maintenance Superintendent"
(janitor)

❖

Not making your
first million by age thirty

$\mathcal{R}$ealizing that you've earned
and spent a million by age fifty

❖

$\mathcal{B}$eing promoted to Manager when
you hate supervising people

❖

$\mathcal{H}$aving to attend a "touchy-feelly"
management-training seminar

$\mathcal{A}$ hugger in your group

❖

"$\mathcal{P}$ower" stuff; e.g.,
lunch, ties, etc.

❖

$\mathcal{T}$he "Suits"

Office size as a
measurement of success

❖

Multi-page application forms
for burger-flipping jobs

❖

Handling smudgy carbon copies
in a company too cheap
to buy a photocopier

That you can't get a buzz
from sniffing Xerox copies

❖

When executives of nearly
bankrupt businesses receive
huge salaries and bonuses

❖

Golden parachutes

Not knowing what color
your parachute is

❖

When a crummy gold
retirement watch is given to
reward thirty-five years of work

❖

Resumes containing
misspelled words

Not hitting your sales target

❖

People playing office politics

❖

Losing at office politics

*I*ndiscreet office romances

❖

*W*hen the rumor mill
picks up news about
your personal peccadilloes

❖

*C*ompanies with high
employee turnover

$\mathcal{P}$laying "musical desks"

❖

$\mathcal{W}$hen your three-year-old
answers your home-office phone

❖

$\mathcal{B}$osses who take credit
for your ideas

Highly paid business gurus

❖

Push-push-push type A bosses

Leaning back too far in your
chair and falling backwards
during a meeting

❖

Having to wear a dorky uniform

The fact that eighty percent
of all job openings are
never advertised

❖

Losing your friends
when you become a boss

Coworkers who never
get your name right

❖

Coworkers who call you "Hon"

❖

"Telecommuters"
goofing off at home

The fact that most
heart attacks occur on Mondays

❖

The practice of
firing people on Fridays

❖

Whoever tightens all the
toilet-paper dispensers every night
so they won't roll freely

$\mathcal{W}$hen a well-paid exec
wins the football pool

❖

$\mathcal{W}$hen someone has an
occupationally appropriate surname;
e.g., a dentist named Dr. Payne

$\mathcal{P}$eople who think a
meteorologist studies meteors

❖

$\mathcal{W}$hen your boss has
a sign on her desk reading
"Thank God It's Monday"

Sitting under a flickering
fluorescent bulb

❖

When easy little jobs that
should have been done last week
pile up into an arduous task

Procrastination

❖

Having a job like Chaplin's in *Modern Times*

Thick volumes of
policies and procedures

❖

Prohibitions against phoning
your spouse from work

"Roach-coach" food trucks

❖

When there's no good place
to go for lunch where you work

❖

Being the last smoker
in your office

Having to work on Saturday

❖

That schools leave you
totally unprepared for working
in the real world

When your brain buzzes from
too many cups of coffee

❖

People who pillage the first-aid
supplies for use at home

The lousy first job that
jaundices your view of work,
like a paper route

❖

People who paper their
cubicle walls with comic strips

$\mathcal{W}$hen everyone in your office
has a "Far Side" mug or calendar

❖

$\mathcal{W}$hen the company hatchet man
wants to see you in private

❖

$\mathcal{W}$hen the boss unexpectedly
joins you and your friends at lunch

Having Friday on
your mind Monday

❖

The extreme scarcity
of job openings for sidekicks
to TV talkshow hosts
and superheroes

Athletes who make more in
ten minutes than you make in a year

❖

Going into business with
a partner named Judas

❖

That success in business is
not about what you know,
but who you know

$\mathcal{N}$ot having any connections

❖

$\mathcal{I}$nheriting an obsolete
family business, like a haberdashery
or a milk-delivery truck

❖

$\mathcal{W}$hen a five-page memo can be
condensed into a simple "No"

Heavy toolbelts that keep
pulling your pants down

❖

Suspecting that "gaffer" is
not a real job, just an inside joke
enjoyed by movie makers

❖

Faxes that never reach
their intended recipients

$\mathcal{P}$eople who use fuzzy
memo phraseology; e.g.,
"It reacted unexpectedly"
instead of "It exploded"

❖

$\mathcal{P}$eople who want to
measure your productivity

Suppliers who never make
deliveries by the promised dates

❖

The last twenty minutes
of the work day

❖

Being told,
"You're not paid to think"

*W*hen you work for
a total butt-head,
wondering what that
makes *you*

❖

*P*eople who come to work with bits
of bloody tissue stuck to their faces

Coworkers who ask "How are you?"
but couldn't care less

❖

Coworkers who *tell you*
when you ask, "How are you?"

❖

The fact that attractive people are
paid more than plain people

$\mathcal{W}$orking with vapid music
playing in the background

❖

$\mathcal{C}$ompany name changes that
render obsolete all your
business cards, stationery, etc.

Coffee mugs imprinted with feeble attempts at office humor

❖

When the boss won't let you write crude comments on his bulletin board memos

When they can trace
your handwriting from your
Suggestion Box submissions

❖

When you don't know if
the "Chris" you're writing a
business letter to is a Mr. or a Ms.

$\mathcal{N}$ever getting promoted because
you're too good at what you do

❖

$\mathcal{W}$orking in a leaky think tank

❖

$\mathcal{A}$ll work and no play

Discovering you're out of
"back-up" underwear while
getting dressed for work

❖

Temps with snotty attitudes
because they know it's
just a temporary job

Knowing *you* could have invented
Liquid Paper, instead of that
dippy Monkee guy's *mom*

❖

Getting sooty copy-machine toner
on your hands and clothes

When the public can
use the employees' rest rooms
where you work

❖

Having only a vague idea
of who owns the conglomerate
you work for

Seeing the company president
only on Christmas eve

❖

People who p*ss and moan
about the high-paying,
high-stress jobs they fought to get

$\mathcal{W}$hen you can't convince
the boss of your need for a
"mental-health day"

❖

$\mathcal{H}$aving to work well into your
ninth month of pregnancy

❖

$\mathcal{C}$lawing and scratching your way
up to the middle

$\mathcal{P}$eople who succeed in business
without really trying

❖

$\mathcal{P}$eople who call their
work a "game";
e.g., "I'm in the pajama game"

Having to contribute cash
every time someone at work
pops out a baby

❖

The lie
"Hard work never killed anyone"

❖

That the Surgeon General
hasn't declared working
hazardous to your health

Bosses who think they're funny

❖

Having to laugh at your
boss's lame jokes

❖

Having to run personal errands
for your boss

$\mathcal{R}$ich people who have never
worked a day in their lives

❖

$\mathcal{P}$eople who want
everything done yesterday

❖

$\mathcal{P}$eople who use
too much job jargon

Corny business clichés like
"Let's run this up the flagpole
and see if anyone salutes"

❖

Department heads who
constantly ask,
"How goes the battle?"

When your friends visit
your fast-food workplace
and expect free food

❖

When friends visit your bank job
and request free samples

Knowing that you'd be
fantastic in a job that
hasn't been invented yet

❖

People who don't quit their jobs
after they win the lottery

Companies that
reorganize frequently

❖

Merging with a company
full of dweebs

❖

Hostile takeovers

"*If* u cn rd ths,
u cn bcm a secty
& gt a gd jb"

❖

Taking shorthand meeting notes
that you can't decipher later

❖

Taking the time to pack a lunch
and then forgetting it at home

The boss's offspring

❖

When someone marries
the boss's offspring and is
given a top position in the company

❖

Working in a family-owned
business when you're not family

$\mathcal{P}$eople who peddle
thigh-reducing cream for a living

❖

$\mathcal{O}$ccupational hazards; e.g.,
mail delivery and dogbites,
piano moving and hernias,
management and ulcers,
parenting and insanity

Coworkers who wear too much perfume or cologne to the office

❖

Business letters that begin, "It has come to my attention . . ."

❖

Business letters that end, "Best regards"

When the company
somehow manages to
stay afloat after you quit

❖

Having many interests,
and being forced to pick just one
as your life's work

❖

People who knew what they
wanted to be by age ten

That there's no welcome mat
to the working world

❖

Job hunting

❖

Pounding the pavement

Ads that say you can
make big money at home
stuffing envelopes

❖

Going to an interview
and being told they'll let you
know in a few days, and never
hearing from them

The catch-22 when you need
experience to get a job, but first
need a job to get experience

❖

Having to give an interviewer
your best phony smile
and heartiest handshake

$\mathcal{D}$iscovering how much gets
deducted from your first paycheck

❖

$\mathcal{W}$hen you stop wondering
what you're going to be
and realize *this is it*

Having to give two weeks' notice
before quitting, when you can get
canned at a moment's notice

❖

Having to share a desk

❖

Sharing a desk with a Madonna buff

Hammering your thumb when
posting the work safety rules

❖

Parental pressure to carry on
the family business

❖

Living in the shadow of a relative
who did some great work

The obnoxious—
but indispensable—employee
whom management can't fire

❖

When you bitch about
the boss to someone at the
company picnic who turns out to
be the boss's daughter

Pay raises lower
than the rate of inflation

❖

Smearing not-quite-dry white-out

❖

Calling in sick on a
Monday or Friday when you
really are sick

Supervisors who have a
hissy fit if you go one minute
over your break

❖

When mature adults are treated
like children as soon as they
enter the factory gates

$\mathcal{H}$eavy manual labor
that makes the twelve labors
of Hercules look easy

❖

$\mathcal{P}$utting your nose to the grindstone

$\mathcal{M}$ates who come home
and always complain about
what a bad day they had

❖

$\mathcal{W}$hen your job leads to a divorce

❖

$\mathcal{H}$aving to scrounge up a date
for an out-of-town client

$\mathcal{P}$eople who blow you off with
"I'm on my break"

❖

$\mathcal{U}$sing up all your personal days
in one week

When you've killed off
all your grandparents for excuses
for days off

❖

The sorry state of a butt that sat
for twenty years behind a desk

Coworkers who remind you
every Wednesday (without fail)
that it's "Hump Day"

❖

Employees who habitually respond,
"Hey, no problem"

$\mathcal{D}$iscovering that you
eventually become like the people
you work with, but hey, no problem

❖

$\mathcal{D}$iscovering that every job takes
at least twice as long as you
initially think it will

When the boss desperately wants
to contact you on the day
you snuck out early

❖

When people at work
call you at home

❖

Executives with showy status
symbols festooning their offices

Professionals who wear
shoes with tassels

❖

When your budget for pencils
gets cut by people who arrive
at work in limos

❖

Jobs employing jackhammers,
or working within earshot of them

Working in a doughnut shop when
you're wanted by the police

❖

Time cards

❖

Having to punch a clock

$\mathcal{W}$ishing you could punch out the
foreman once in a while

❖

$\mathcal{H}$aving to moonlight

❖

$\mathcal{M}$oonlighting as a kids' party clown
and not being able to write off
the seltzer bottles

Coworkers who snap you
with rubber bands

❖

Managers who retire on-the-job

❖

Being the token anything
in the office

Wondering whether your
building's elevator-repair person
was an A or a C student

❖

Knowing that even God didn't want
to work seven days straight

$\mathcal{B}$eing named
employee of the month
instead of getting a raise

❖

$\mathcal{B}$eing a writer with
no connections in the
publishing business

Watching a triple-overtime game at 1:00 A.M. when you have to get up for work at 5:00 A.M.

❖

So-called workshops in which you neither work nor shop

❖

The company muckety-mucks, bigwigs, and pooh-bahs

$\mathcal{P}$eople who "do lunch"

❖

$\mathcal{P}$eople who "take a meeting"

❖

$\mathcal{W}$hen a subordinate gets your job

Getting hungry while
making a pie chart

❖

Pen and pencil sets
with unsharpenable pencils

❖

Wondering why a painting is
called a work of art

Wondering why a
grungy factory is called a plant

❖

Discovering you could have
gotten your job through
a matchbook cover instead of
four years of college

When your desk drawer derails

❖

When a file cabinet slams
shut on your finger

❖

Having to dress exactly
like everyone else

Having to sing a little company
song before work begins

❖

When a three-ring binder
nips your finger

❖

Being accused of
having a bad attitude

When your hobby becomes
collecting unemployment checks

❖

People who list fake Ivy League
degrees on their resumes and
don't get caught

❖

Scheduled rest room breaks

Staggered lunch breaks

❖

People who stagger back to work
after a "liquid lunch"

❖

Companies that don't
believe in flextime

Doing no-brainer work that could
be performed by a chimp

❖

When a chimp gets your job,
and does it better

❖

Executives who never eat in
the company cafeteria

$\mathcal{R}$eserved parking spots for
the company's big shots

❖

$\mathcal{P}$eople with signs on
their office doors proclaiming
who they are

❖

$\mathcal{W}$hen your company's
medical insurance plan
can be summed up in three words:
"Don't get sick"

$\mathcal{N}$eeding to fill out a form to get
anything accomplished

❖

$\mathcal{W}$hen you run out
of the form that must be used
to order more forms

❖

$\mathcal{T}$he unreadably light bottom page
of multi-page forms

When your kid has to write
a school essay on
"What My Mommy and Daddy Do"
and draws a blank

❖

That you just can't get
good help these days

Job applicants who start
their interviews by
asking about vacations

❖

When employers forget
"you get what you pay for"

❖

MBAs in BMWs

Being unemployed on Labor Day

❖

Getting laid off at Christmastime

❖

Getting drenched when replacing
the water-cooler bottle

The fact that tall people are
paid more than short

❖

The fact that fat people
earn less than thin

❖

Hanging out too much with the
office trivia maven

Bosses who never socialize
with their employees

❖

Signs that read
"Will Work for Food
(and $65,000 a year)"

❖

Days that make you wish you
had run away with the circus

$\mathcal{W}$hen an employee
goes over your head

❖

$\mathcal{B}$eing badgered by headhunters

❖

$\mathcal{P}$eople who watch the soaps
every day on the lunch room TV

When "a bonus" is a
foreign phrase where you work

❖

When you work through lunch,
but aren't allowed to leave
an hour early

❖

People who come to work sick,
so you can catch whatever they have

$\mathcal{W}$hen you can't afford
to stay out sick

❖

"$\mathcal{F}$ire-proof" government workers

❖

$\mathcal{U}$nions for Elvis impersonators

$\mathcal{J}$obs that look easy
until you try to do them

❖

$\mathcal{A}$lways flying by the
seat of your pants

❖

$\mathcal{W}$hen the boss flies first class
and makes you go coach

$\mathcal{L}$ooking for a workplace that
brings back the feeling of playing
in a vacant lot as a child

❖

$\mathcal{W}$hen everyone at work is
rowing in a different direction

❖

$\mathcal{W}$hen your photography business
just doesn't click

When no one gets
your jokes at work

❖

Celebrities who bitch about how
hard it is to be rich and famous

❖

When your boss finds the
resume you accidentally left
on the copy machine

Budget cuts

❖

Coworkers who clip
their nails at their desks

❖

Flying nail clippings landing
on your desk

Having to play golf
to get ahead in your job

❖

That lawyers don't have to worry
about giving their profession
a bad name

❖

Naive workers who have the
notion that a company owes them
more than a paycheck

$\mathcal{B}$eing part of an orchestra
when you're a one-man-band
kind of person

❖

$\mathcal{B}$oring graffiti-free restroom walls

❖

$\mathcal{C}$oworkers who don't flush

The forced cheerfulness of
Disneyland employees

❖

SWAT teams that do squat

❖

Receiving junk faxes

Riding to work in a
steamy, packed subway car

❖

When conductors make
cute announcements over the
subway's P.A. system

❖

When coworkers find out
how much you make

Growing poor slowly
instead of getting rich quick

❖

People who do the work of
two men—Laurel and Hardy

❖

Being categorized by
the color of your collar:
white, blue, pink, etc.

Not being told what happened to
the previous holder of your job

❖

Seeing your best ideas wind up
in the "circular file"

❖

Cold calling

Door-to-door selling

❖

"How to Succeed" books
written by losers

❖

Wheelers and dealers

$\mathcal{M}$easuring out your days
in coffee spoons

❖

$\mathcal{P}$eople who play little tunes on
their touch-tone phones

❖

$\mathcal{B}$eing computer-phobic in
a high-tech profession

People who discuss
work while at home

❖

People who discuss
work during sex

The lack of real communication at work, despite all the sophisticated technology used, such as phones, faxes, PCs, etc.

❖

Stupid managerial decisions that cost hundreds of people their jobs

When the only group you join is
the hard-core unemployed

❖

Living paycheck to paycheck

❖

When you need to make
1,000 copies immediately,
and the machine is in 500 pieces,
spread out on the floor

When your boss gives you that
"Are you out of your mind?" look

❖

Trying to soar with the eagles
when you work with turkeys

❖

People with clean desks

Social security deductions
when you're young

❖

Employees who shape up two weeks
before their performance reviews

❖

Leaders who couldn't lead a pack
of hungry wolves to meat

$\mathcal{W}$hen the human cannonball gets
fired because he's the wrong caliber

❖

$\mathcal{B}$ouncing paychecks

❖

$\mathcal{W}$hen the company's CEO
is younger than you

That no one will tell you the truth
once you put on a tie

❖

Having to use your vacation days
to cover an extended illness

❖

The greeting card company that
invented Bosses' Day

Feeling like an easily replaceable
part in a big machine

❖

When the paper trail
leads back to you

❖

Having a dream in which you go to
work in your underwear

That it's always a "bad time"
in the business you're
trying to break into

❖

Personnel departments that say
they'll keep your resume on file

❖

When it seems like no job
could be worse than yours

$\mathcal{D}$ismal positions, like
Urinal Cigarette-Butt Retriever . . .

❖

. . . $\mathcal{H}$ospital Bed-Pan Washer . . .

❖

. . . $\mathcal{P}$erson Who Plucks Those
Last Three Little Hairs
From Chicken Legs . . .

. . . *J*oke Writer for
former senator Bob Dole . . .

❖

. . . *O*r the person who mops
floors in a porno theater

❖

*B*eing paid peanuts if you're
not a pachyderm

When there's no sugar
or cream for coffee

❖

Bosses who want you to
call problems opportunities

❖

Having to prove yourself
in a new job

$\mathcal{P}$eople who count down the
days until their retirement

❖

$\mathcal{H}$aving a boss like Mr. Dithers
in the comic strip "Blondie"

❖

$\mathcal{A}$cquiring an unattractive slouch
from years of sitting

That the higher you go in an organization, the smaller your briefcase gets

❖

Feeling too pooped after work to do what you had been looking forward to all day

Hitting every red light when
you're late for work

❖

The millions of people unhappy
in their jobs

❖

Glum receptionists

No appreciation for the
superhuman effort you exert daily
just to show up at work

❖

Working at breakneck speed
eight hours a day to get
to be a boss working
furiously twelve hours a day

$\mathcal{P}$eople who nibble and chip away
at their foam coffee cups

❖

$\mathcal{D}$riving to work on "auto-pilot"
and not remembering a thing
about the ride

❖

$\mathcal{B}$osses who believe that all
employees are basically lazy slugs

Employees who believe
that all bosses are
basically manipulative slimeballs

❖

Getting chewed out
in front of coworkers

❖

Quitting your job before
getting a new one

Begging your old job to take you back when a new job doesn't work out

❖

When your lemonade stand sales go sour

❖

Having two years of experience in five jobs, instead of ten years of experience in one job

Having to explain tactfully why
you "left" your last job

❖

When they discharge you summarily,
but give you a glowing letter
of recommendation

❖

When you're the one who always
brings in the morning doughnuts

Having to buy holiday gifts
for your coworkers

❖

That the greater the risk,
the greater the reward

❖

Coworkers who quit,
started their own businesses,
and succeeded wildly

Being stuck in a go-nowhere job

❖

A job that doesn't use
any of your talents

❖

Overnight packages that
arrive a day late

Having to copy letter-size
documents on legal-size paper,
then chop it

❖

When your paper cutter
makes ragged edges

❖

Confusing the terms "inter-office"
and "intra-office"

259

People who insist their way is
the only right way to do a job

❖

Growing old disgracefully
on your job

❖

Plant closures

Strikes and lockouts

❖

Walking on a picket line

❖

Companies that don't
provide child care

Being terminated because
your boss woke up on the wrong side
of the bed that day

❖

When your tie gets caught
in the fax machine and you send
yourself to the West Coast

The lack of appreciation for the
amount of work a baby does
in its first year

❖

Calling hookers "sex workers"

❖

Discovering that you've been in
the wrong field for years

Being the only public school
graduate in an office full
of Ivy Leaguers

❖

People who lust
after the corner office

❖

Never having an office
with a window

$\mathcal{B}$osses who sit in a chair
a little higher than everybody else's

❖

$\mathcal{W}$hen your earning power
has peaked

❖

$\mathcal{G}$etting splinters on your
slide down the corporate ladder

The demise of craftsmanship
and pride in work

❖

That the best-quality American car
now equals the worst-quality
Japanese car

❖

Taxi drivers with Ph.D.'s

The silent realization that
there are others better
suited for your job

❖

When all your coworkers
smell your microwave popcorn
and want some

Having to say something nice
about the boss's god-awful entry
in the employee art show

❖

People who confuse
a memo with reality

❖

People with "can't-do" attitudes

Mattress-testers
lying down on the job

❖

Awakening in the small hours of
the morning, thinking about work

❖

Forever searching for your
elusive "dream job"

$\mathcal{N}$ot heeding Thoreau's
warning about "any enterprise
requiring new clothes"

❖

$\mathcal{S}$taples jammed in your stapler

❖

$\mathcal{L}$avish executive perks

$\mathcal{N}$ot having a key to
the executive washroom

❖

$\mathcal{C}$orporate belt-tightening, when
only employees feel the pinch

❖

$\mathcal{T}$hat "the bigger they are,
the harder they fall"
doesn't apply in business

Being told something unfair
is company policy

❖

The sink-or-swim method
of job training

❖

The fact that you have to work
until mid-May just to pay taxes

$\mathcal{B}$eing ashamed to speak at your
kid's Career Day class because
you don't do something flashy

❖

$\mathcal{M}$issing your life's calling

❖

$\mathcal{G}$oing back to work
after a long absence

$\mathcal{B}$eing introduced as
"someone who fancies himself a
(writer, artist, etc.)"

❖

$\mathcal{C}$ustomers who demand
preferential treatment because of
who they are or who they know

Coworkers who are forever
conducting personal business
over the phone

❖

How people who do things
they enjoy seem to live a long time

The fact that actuaries
have the lowest stress jobs

❖

When your cellular phone fades out

❖

Undated correspondence

That there never seems
to be enough time to do
the things you want to do

❖

Jobs that get no respect; e.g.,
cop, shopping mall guard,
baby-sitter, gas station attendant,
supermarket checker, editor

That no one on his deathbed
ever wished he'd spent more time
at the office

❖

When your job's no fun anymore

❖

Paper cuts on your tongue
from licking envelopes

That a mother's work
is never done

❖

The piercing screech your
file drawer makes every time
you open it

❖

Realizing too late that files,
desks, and machines won't keep
you warm at night

Forgetting to enjoy the scenery
on your journey through
the working world

❖

When you don't stop and
smell the roses sometimes

❖

When your boss calls you into
his office and there's a copy
of this book in his hand